KIDS ON EARTH

Wildlife Adventures – Explore The World
Leopard Shark - Maldives

Sensei Paul David

COPYRIGHT PAGE

Kids On Earth: Wildlife Adventures - Explore The World

Leopard Shark - Maldives

by Sensei Paul David,

Copyright © 2023.

All rights reserved.

978-1-77848-195-6 KoE_WildLife_Amazon_PaperbackBook_maldives_leopard shark

978-1-77848-194-9 KoE_WildLife_Amazon_eBook_maldives_leopard shark

978-1-77848-427-8 KoE_Wildlife_Ingram_Paperbackbook_LeopardShark

This book is not authorized for free distribution copying.

www.senseipublishing.com

@senseipublishing
#senseipublishing

Synopsis

This non-fiction book for children aged 6 to 12 introduces the unique Leopard Shark, a species of hound shark found in the waters of the Maldives. It describes the physical characteristics, behavior, and habitat of the Leopard Shark, and provides 30 fun facts about the species. The book also discusses the importance of the Leopard Shark to the ecosystem of the Maldives, its role in the local economy, and the need to conserve and protect the species and its habitat.

Get Our FREE Books Now!

kidsonearth.life

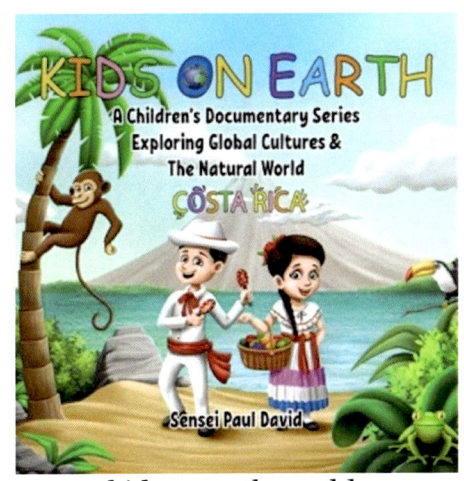

kidsonearth.world

Click Below for Another Book In Each Series

senseipublishing.com/KoE_SERIES

senseipublishing.com/KoE_Wildlife_SERIES

KoE En Español

senseipublishing.com/KoE_SERIES_SPANISH

www.senseipublishing.com

Join Our Publishing Journey!

If you would like to receive FUTURE FREE BOOKS and get to know us better, please click www.senseipublishing.com and join our newsletter by entering your email address in the pop-up box.

Follow Our Blog: senseipauldavid.ca

Follow/Like/Subscribe: Facebook, Instagram, YouTube: @senseipublishing

Scan the QR Code with your phone or tablet to follow us on social media:

Like / Subscribe / Follow

Introduction

Welcome to the fascinating world of the Leopard Shark! This book will take you on a journey to the beautiful Maldives, a country located in the Indian Ocean, and introduce you to this unique species of shark. You will learn about the physical characteristics of the Leopard Shark, its behavior, and its habitat. You will also discover some fun facts about this amazing creature that will excite and delight children ages 6 to 12. So dive in and learn all about the Leopard Shark!

The Leopard Shark is a species of hound shark and is a type of ground shark.

It is named for its spotted pattern of dark and light spots, which resemble the hide of a leopard.

The Leopard Shark is found in the waters of the Maldives, an island nation in the Indian Ocean.

The Leopard Shark can grow up to a length of 7 feet (2.13 meters).

It has a slender body with a long snout and large eyes.

The Leopard Shark has sharp, pointed teeth and a strong jaw.

It feeds mainly on small fish, crabs, and invertebrates.

The Leopard Shark is usually found in shallow, coastal waters and can often be seen swimming close to the surface.

It is a slow swimmer and prefers to cruise through the water.

The Leopard Shark is an ovoviviparous species, meaning that the embryos develop inside the mother's body and are born live.

The mother can give birth to up to 25 pups at a time.

The Leopard Shark is an important part of the food chain in the Maldives, providing food for larger predators such as sharks and other fish.

The Leopard Shark is not considered a threat to humans and is harmless.

The Leopard Shark is a popular target for recreational fishing in the Maldives.

The average lifespan of the Leopard Shark is around 15 years.

The Leopard Shark is a protected species in the Maldives and fishing for them is strictly prohibited.

The Leopard Shark is a popular attraction for scuba divers and snorkelers in the Maldives.

The Leopard Shark is usually found in groups, and can sometimes be seen "herding" together.

The Leopard Shark is an ambush predator, meaning that it will hide and wait until the perfect moment to strike its prey.

The Leopard Shark is nocturnal, meaning that it is most active at night.

The Leopard Shark has excellent eyesight and can detect its prey from a distance.

The Leopard Shark is an important part of the ocean's ecosystem, helping to keep the waters clean and healthy.

The Leopard Shark has a special organ in its body called the ampullae of Lorenzini, which is sensitive to electrical fields in the water.

The Leopard Shark has a unique form of communication called "body language", which it uses to communicate with other sharks.

The Leopard Shark is a migratory species, meaning that it moves from one area to another in search of food and mates.

The Leopard Shark has been known to travel long distances, up to thousands of miles, in search of food and mates.

The Leopard Shark is extremely sensitive to changes in the environment, such as temperature and pollution.

The Leopard Shark is an important part of the local economy of the Maldives, as it is an important part of the tourist industry.

The Leopard Shark is a social species and can often be seen swimming with other sharks.

The Leopard Shark is an important part of the ocean's food web and helps to maintain a healthy and balanced ecosystem.

Conclusion

We hope you have enjoyed learning about the amazing Leopard Shark! This unique species of shark is an important part of the ecosystem in the Maldives, providing food for larger predators and helping to keep the waters clean and healthy. The Leopard Shark is also an important part of the local economy, as it is a popular attraction for recreational fishing and scuba diving. We hope that you have enjoyed learning about this fascinating species and that you have been inspired to help conserve and protect the Leopard Shark and its habitat for future generations.

Thank you for reading this book!

If you found this book helpful, I would be grateful if you would **post an honest review on Amazon** so this book can reach other supportive readers like you!

All you need to do is digitally flip to the back and leave your review. Or visit amazon.com/author/senseipauldavid click the correct book cover and click on the blue link next to the yellow stars that say, "customer reviews."

As always...

It's a great day to be alive!

Share Our FREE eBooks Now!

kidsonearth.life

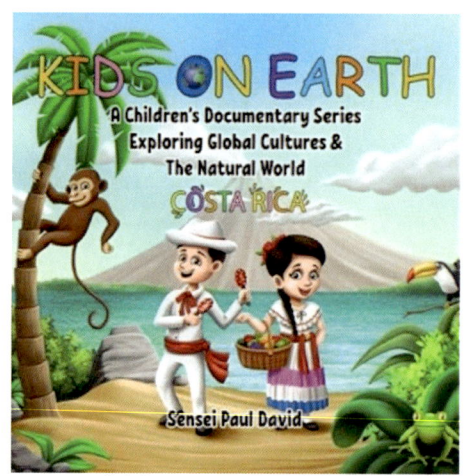

kidsonearth.world

Click Below for Another Book In Each Series

senseipublishing.com/KoE_SERIES

senseipublishing.com/KoE_Wildlife_SERIES

KoE En Español

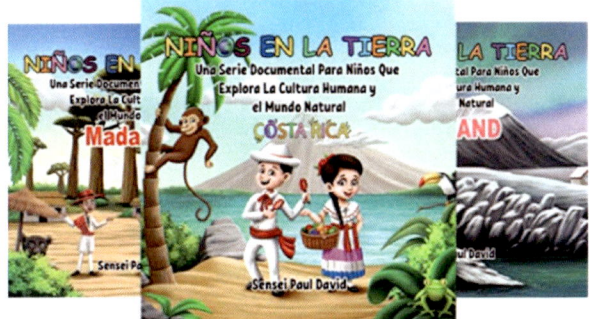

senseipublishing.com/KoE_SERIES_SPANISH

www.senseipublishing.com

www.senseipublishing.com

@senseipublishing
#senseipublishing

Check out our **recommendations** for other books for adults & kids plus other great resources by visiting
www.senseipublishing.com/resources/

Join Our Publishing Journey!

If you would like to receive FREE BOOKS and special offers, please visit www.senseipublishing.com and join our newsletter by entering your email address in the pop-up box

Follow Our Engaging Blog NOW!
senseipauldavid.ca

Get Our FREE Books Today!

Click & Share the Links Below

FREE Kids Books

lifeofbailey.senseipublishing.com
kidsonearth.senseipublishing.com

FREE Self-Development Book

senseiselfdevelopment.senseipublishing.com

FREE BONUS!!!
Experience Over 25 FREE Engaging Guided Meditations!

Prized Skills & Practices for Adults & Kids. Help Restore Deep Sleep, Lower Stress, Improve Posture, Navigate Uncertainty & More.

Download the Free Insight Timer App and click the link below:
http://insig.ht/sensei_paul

About Sensei Publishing

Sensei Publishing commits itself to helping people of all ages transform into better versions of themselves by providing high-quality and research-based self-development books with an emphasis on mental health and guided meditations. Sensei Publishing offers well-written e-books, audiobooks, paperbacks, and online courses that simplify complicated but practical topics in line with its mission to inspire people toward positive transformation.

It's a great day to be alive!

About the Author

I create simple & transformative eBooks & Guided Meditations for Adults & Children proven to help navigate uncertainty, solve niche problems & bring families closer together.

I'm a former finance project manager, private pilot, jiu-jitsu instructor, musician & former University of Toronto Fitness Trainer. I prefer a science-based approach to focus on these & other areas in my life to stay humble & hungry to evolve. I hope you enjoy my work and I'd love to hear your feedback.

- It's a great day to be alive!
Sensei Paul David

Scan & Follow/Like/Subscribe: Facebook, Instagram, YouTube: @senseipublishing

Scan using your phone/iPad camera for Social Media
Visit us at www.senseipublishing.com and sign up for our newsletter to learn more about our exciting books and to experience our FREE Guided Meditations for Kids & Adults.

www.ingramcontent.com/pod-product-compliance
Lightning Source LLC
Chambersburg PA
CBRC090902080526
44587CB00008B/169